Stand Out As A Speaker & #Be More Giraffe

Elliot Kay

ISBN: 978-1-5272-9601-5

Designed by Danny&co.
Illustration by Frances Hashmi.

FOR MY KIDS, FAMILY AND TO ANYONE WHO WANTS TO MAKE THIS WORLD A BETTER PLACE, BE SEEN BE HEARD AND ALWAYS BE MORE GIRAFFE

"I loved it. I found it very clear to read & powerful. I like that it doesn't take long to read and lists key points to implement to stand out immediately"
Susan Stocker, *Law of Attraction Life Coach*

"After reading this practical, engaging, and fun book, I choose to stand out and grab attention within this crowded and noisy marketplace by fully embracing the #bemoregiraffe structure and philosophy."
Jose Ucar, *Communications Expert*

"How To Stand Out As A Speaker & #BeMoreGiraffe is a brilliant book, with so many valuable, memorable soundbites and great illustrations to remind us of the power of speaking, how to communicate through our authentic, personal voice, and how to craft a profile and message that genuinely helps us stand out from our competition and rise above the noise. Filled with practical tips and humour, this is a must read for everyone who wants to develop their personal brand and attract exactly the right clients for them to succeed."
Jane Bayler Mentor, *Ideal Client Success*

CONTENTS

WHY NOW, YOU MUST BE MORE GIRAFFE

By Elliot Kay

Certainty is one of our greatest human needs.

The events of 2020 leading into 2021 have created an unprecedented challenge to our much needed certainty. During such times, as humans we have a habit of retracting, of pulling back, of 'protecting ourselves'. This is an entirely normal response, in fact one which we depend on as a race for our survival. It is our instinct to remain safe – even if this is a perceived safety created in our minds, when in reality we are creating further discomfort and uncertainty in the long term.

Our survival instincts also tell us to be part of a tribe, 'safety in numbers', blend in, follow what others are doing. Be 'vanilla'. We fear being different. We believe being like others will provide us with the acceptance we so crave and need to provide that safety net around us. This will keep us safe and comfortable. It will give us certainty. In the short term.

What we fail to do as we strive to regain some short-term control and safety, is to consider opportunities that we could be creating. We fail to remember that rarely do great things happen from the zone of safety or over night.

Regardless of your industry, opportunities exist, you just need to be open to seeing them or seeking them out. We need to adapt. We need to think in a different way. Show up in a different way, be seen and heard in a different way.

We need to consider that maybe standing out, rather than joining in, is in fact the better strategy to achieve our goals. We need to #bemoregiraffe.

We can create stability from what we have the potential to create as opposed to shying away from it. As we navigate our way through the uncertainty that the last few months have brought us, we have the opportunity to answer a very powerful question: Join in or stand out? Which do you choose?

A giraffe will stand head and shoulders above others, it will stick its neck out. It won't blend into the background unless it has to and as such it earns the title of one of the most amazing creatures in its habitat. It is respected for its uniqueness.

Let's think about the crowded online space, which is a frustration cited by most of my clients at the moment. But first, imagine a busy market for a moment. One where you can't hear what the vendors are saying, as each is shouting louder, trying to be heard in order to sell their produce. Sure, you might go to the stand with the lowest price for your strawberries but most likely you will go to the stand that grabs your attention.

Maybe it's their layout, maybe the way the vendor is interacting, maybe they make you laugh, maybe they make it very clear what they are selling,  removing any questions from your mind. Maybe you go to the vendor that sells no other produce but only specialises in strawberries. Sounds like a risky tactic but it means they are an expert in their produce. It can be an interesting exercise to consider your own purchasing decisions and what leads you to make them – often not on a conscious level. Because behind that vendor is a giraffe that somehow said or did the right thing to capture your attention.

Right now, we are all vendors as much as we are all buyers and on the whole we all have one single market place: the internet.

As entrepreneurs, it is more important than ever to therefore define that specific message that will compel your clients and to communicate with them in a way that allows you to stand out by using your own tone – not by trying to shout louder above everyone else. We all need to be clear about who we are, what we stand for and that clarity will be rewarded by the connection and trust from your clients.

Remember we all want certainty, so an offer that leaves any room for doubt is an offer that will stay on the table. Fact!

The starting point of being more giraffe is about that message. It's about thinking about what makes us relatable. What makes us vulnerable. We need to be prepared to alienate many people in order to reach the right client – if our message is so niche that it only reaches 1% of the population, that is still a huge audience to serve.

So before simply throwing more energy and resources into marketing and advertising, ask yourself:

- What makes me stand out?
- Who am I really trying to engage?
- How clearly am I communicating exactly what problem I solve and who I help?

Then and only then can your message be amplified with consistent content, like the arms of an octopus; reaching out via different channels,  yet being led by the main body which has a clear core message. Create different touch points for your audience to hear your message in different ways, different platforms, different formats – but always the same consistent message. It has been shown time and time again that a client needs many many touch points before they are ready to buy.

Are you being more giraffe and putting your neck out there to be seen over and over? To be remembered? To influence how you make someone feel even well after they see your content?

This book isn't another 'nice to read inspiring book before I go back to being an ostrich'. In this book I have distilled the key insights of the #bemoregiraffe approach for you to refer to again and again and even share the wisdom via your social media channels. I kept it simple and easy. After all it is about #bemoregiraffe, therefore the book needed to be different in itself.

When you get to the end, make sure you take action that makes the giraffe in you stand out.

Look at your message.

Is it fully clear?
Does it stand you out?

Post something that you feel would be more giraffe and use the hashtag
#bemoregiraffe and tag us on instagram
@Stand_out_academy

Take action and do what most wouldn't in order to get the results that most won't.

Because right now it's about being seen, being heard and #bemoregiraffe. Stick your neck out. Be head and shoulders above the rest. And rise above the noise.

Always #bemoregiraffe

Be More Giraffe

WHEN YOU USE YOUR VOICE FOR
GOOD AND SPEAK FOR A HIGHER
PURPOSE YOUR CONFIDENCE IS
IMMEDIATELY ELEVATED

WHEN YOU ARE ABLE TO GRAB ATTENTION WITH YOUR MESSAGE WITHIN 30 SECONDS OR LESS, YOU WILL STAND ABOVE THE REST

Use this structure to nail your 30 second core message.

We/I Know _____

The Problem _____

Our/my solution is _____

Which results in _____

WHEN YOU HAVE A SIGNATURE TALK THAT YOU DELIVER WITH AMAZING STORIES, IMPACT AND PASSION PEOPLE WILL BUY FROM YOU

Use this signature talk structure

Strong opening

3 big problems you address in the talk

Earn The Right
State Your expertise

Solution
What's your unique system/process/service

Story
Choose the appropriate story to tell here

Content
This is your best stuff to educate the audience

Call To Action
State the next natural step for the customer to carry on working with you

BE SO RELEVANT, ENGAGING AND EASILY BOOKABLE THAT EVERYTHING ELSE IS A FORMALITY

Make sure your speaker tool kit is up to date and on point!

Relevant content

Strong Footage

Relevant Images

Strong Speaker Bio

An ability to pitch

Bags of passion

Consistency

WHEN YOU ADD ENOUGH VALUE AND SOLVE MEANINGFUL PROBLEMS - PEOPLE BUY

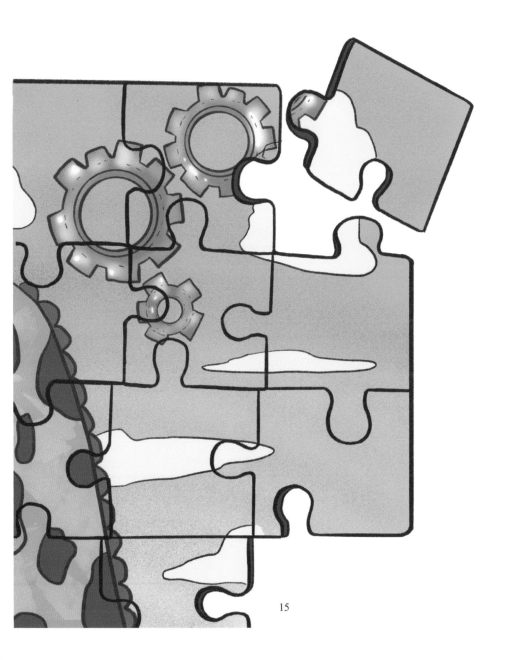

STAGE TIME IS WEALTH TIME

When you can get on as many stages (virtual or offline) as possible, when you add enough value, when you care enough about a community and connect with their heart, you will make a dent in your industry

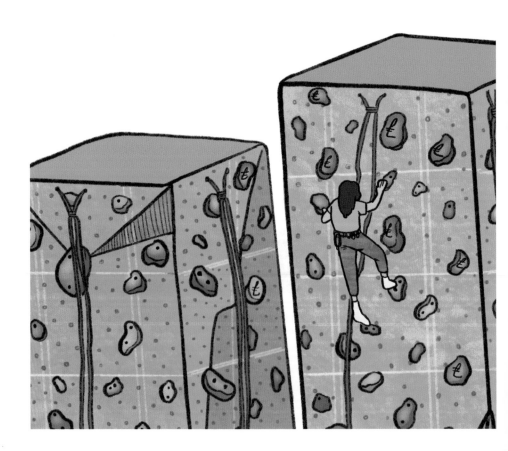

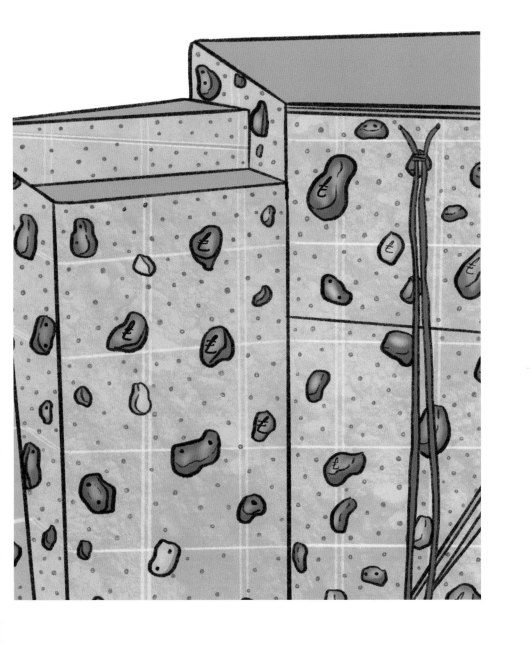

PASSION IS NOT ENOUGH

PASSION WILL ONLY GET YOU SO FAR

PURPOSE WILL GIVE YOU
L O N G E V I T Y

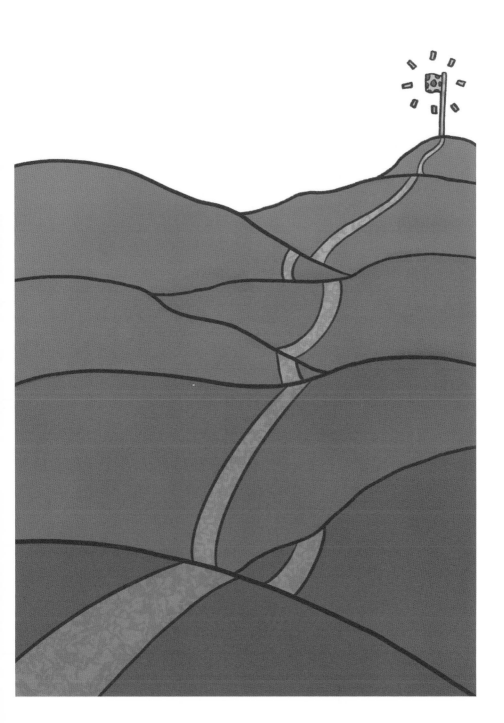

**IN ORDER TO STAND OUT,
STOP FITTING IN**

BEING BRAVE AND BOLD DOESN'T MEAN BEING LOUD AND OBNOXIOUS

INVEST IN YOUR GIRAFFENESS
BECAUSE YOU ARE WORTH IT!

TAKE THE TEST

CHECK OUT THE LAST PAGE, WHEN
YOU HAVE READ EVERYTHING OF

COURSE 😉

8 IMPACT PRINCIPLES
A Speaking Philosophy in order to #bemoregiraffe

1

STAGE TIME - OF COURSE!

Someone invites you to speak, offers you their stage or looks for a volunteer in the audience. Your answer is always 'OF COURSE'. Take every chance – drop every fear.

#bemoregiraffe

2

DARE TO BOMB

We learn from failure NOT success. Be afraid of not giving it a GO. Feedback is never personal anyway - performance, feedback, revision, repeat.

#bemoregiraffe

3

IT'S NOT ABOUT ME

It's about your big WHY, it's about 'falling from your head into your heart'. Once you realise you are on stage to be of service and not to let your doubtful voices get in the way, your nerves will vanish.

#bemoregiraffe

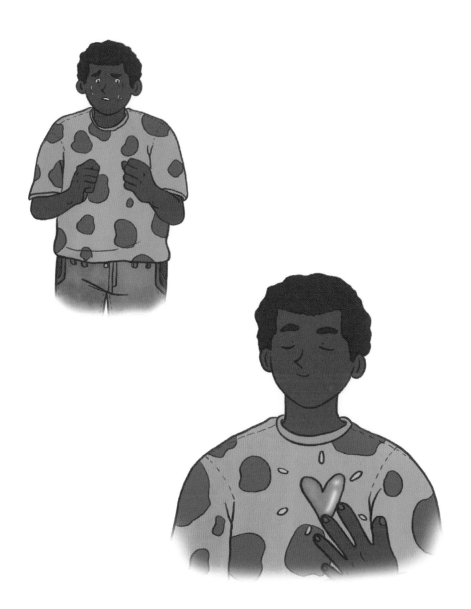

4

WITH VULNERABILITY COMES POWER

Vulnerability is the most accurate measurement of courage. Our imperfections are marks of authenticity and that's the beauty of humanity. Let yourself be seen. Be you.

#bemoregiraffe

5

THE 3 MOST DANGEROUS WORDS: 'I KNOW THAT.'

Our mind is like a parachute, it works best when open! Have you let 'knowing' something stop you from hearing it again? – knowing versus owning. Bite your tongue and be open. Become a master learner to become a master at Impact!

#bemoregiraffe

6

ALWAYS PLAY AT 111%

Dare to go too far! Playing small means you're comfortable, but not memorable. Greatness doesn't come from playing small.

#bemoregiraffe

7

REPETITION CREATES MASTERY

Practise and train. Be on top of your game daily.
Watch other speakers. Be hungry for coaching.
Practise and train some more.

#bemoregiraffe

8

TAKE RESPONSIBILITY & TRACK YOUR PROGRESS

There are only two options: make progress or make excuses. If the opportunity doesn't exist: create it! Your success depends on what you put in.

#bemoregiraffe

**VISUALISE WHAT YOU WILL BECOME BY
COLOURING THIS IMAGE AND
#BEMOREGIRAFFE**

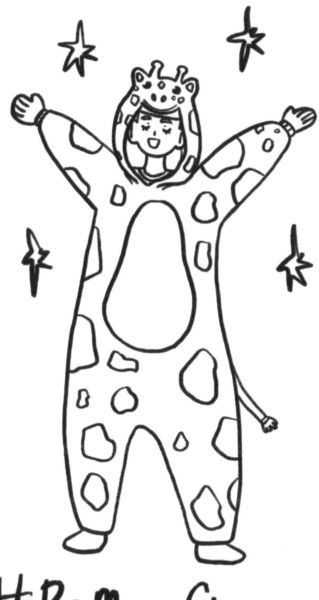

#Be More Giraffe

Now you have coloured it in, send your work or tag us ⓘ @Stand_Out_Academy   #bemoregiraffe

SOME TIPS TO HELP YOU
#BEMOREGIRAFFE DAILY

✦ Spend 30 minutes a day connecting with people you want to speak for – invest in building long lasting relationships.

✦ Practise your talk – even when you don't have any bookings – at least three times a week.

✦ Get mentoring – reach out to us – we got your back.

✦ Get training on a monthly basis. To be world class you must invest in your craft.

✦ Once a week, buy lunch for someone who can be a potential partner/supporter of yours.

✦ Post on social media consistently in a way that gets you noticed…#bemoregiraffe with everything you post.

✦ Dare to have an opinion, share it, share it some more and then share it again. Stand for something!

✦ Always use your voice for good.

✦ Produce exciting and enticing content to draw in people who can and will invite you to speak.

✦ Join our Facebook Group – Stand Out To Win Business.

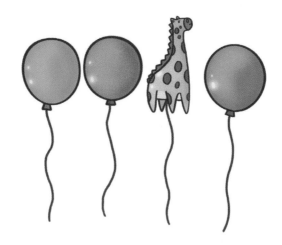

ARE YOU BEING MORE GIRAFFE
WITH YOUR SPEAKING?

Take the test

Scan me

Find out how influential you are as a speaker
Get your personalised score
Get an 18 page report full of even more tips to improve

Printed in Great Britain
by Amazon